Rain Forest Life

Plants of the Rain Forest

by Julie Murray

Dash!
LEVELED READERS
An Imprint of Abdo Zoom • abdobooks.com

Dash!
LEVELED READERS

Level 1 – Beginning
Short and simple sentences with familiar words or patterns for children who are beginning to understand how letters and sounds go together.

Level 2 – Emerging
Longer words and sentences with more complex language patterns for readers who are practicing common words and letter sounds.

Level 3 – Transitional
More developed language and vocabulary for readers who are becoming more independent.

THIS BOOK CONTAINS RECYCLED MATERIALS

abdobooks.com

Published by Abdo Zoom, a division of ABDO, PO Box 398166, Minneapolis, Minnesota 55439.
Copyright © 2023 by Abdo Consulting Group, Inc. International copyrights reserved in all countries.
No part of this book may be reproduced in any form without written permission from the publisher.
Dash!™ is a trademark and logo of Abdo Zoom.

Printed in the United States of America, North Mankato, Minnesota.
102022
012023

Photo Credits: Getty Images, Shutterstock
Production Contributors: Kenny Abdo, Jennie Forsberg, Grace Hansen, John Hansen
Design Contributors: Candice Keimig, Neil Klinepier

Library of Congress Control Number: 2022937229

Publisher's Cataloging in Publication Data

Names: Murray, Julie, author.
Title: Plants of the rain forest / by Julie Murray
Description: Minneapolis, Minnesota : Abdo Zoom, 2023 | Series: Rain forest life | Includes online
    resources and index.
Identifiers: ISBN 9781098280116 (lib. bdg.) | ISBN 9781098280642 (ebook) | ISBN 9781098280949
    (Read-to-Me ebook)
Subjects: LCSH: Rain forest plants--Juvenile literature. | Rain forests--Juvenile literature. | Temperate rain
    forest ecology--Juvenile literature. | Biotic communities--Juvenile literature.
Classification: DDC 577.34--dc23

Table of Contents

Plants of the Rain Forest

More than half of the world's plant **species** grow in rain forests.

From the moss on trees to tall **palms**, each plant is an important part of its **ecosystem**.

Tropical Rain Forest Plants

Palms are the most common plant found in tropical rain forests. Acai palms grow dark purple berries.

Orchids are also common in tropical rain forests. Some kinds of orchids grow on trees.

11

Cacao trees grow large fruit. Inside the fruit are cocao seeds. The seeds are **superfoods**! They are also used to make chocolate.

13

Many other fruits grow in tropical rain forests. Bananas, coconuts, and pineapples are just a few.

15

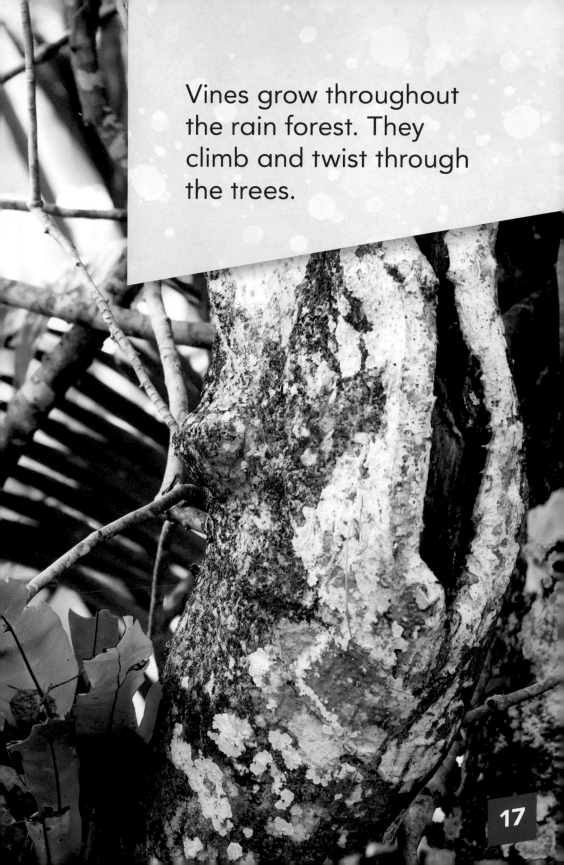

Vines grow throughout the rain forest. They climb and twist through the trees.

Temperate Rain Forest Plants

bigleaf maple

Sitka spruce

Many different trees grow in temperate rain forests. The most common include bigleaf maple, Sitka spruce, and Douglas-fir.

Plants such as ferns, mosses, and **lichens** can grow on other plants. They are often found on tree trunks and branches. Some can even grow on rocks.

More Facts

- Some plants have sharp edges or a bad taste. These defenses keep animals from eating them.

- The Amazon rainforest has more types of plants than any other place on Earth.

- Around 25% of today's Western medicines come from rain forest plants.

Glossary

ecosystem – a community of living things, together with their environment.

lichen – a living thing that is a fungus and a form of algae or special bacteria living together. They live on rocks or other places where there is no soil.

palm – any of a group of tropical plants. Most palms are trees without branches that are topped by crowns of large leaves shaped like feathers.

species – a group of living things that look alike and can have young with one another.

superfood – a food that is rich in compounds (such as antioxidants, fiber, or fatty acids) considered good for a person's health.

Index

ferns 20

flowers 10

fruits 8, 13, 14

lichens 20

moss 6, 20

temperate rain forest 19

trees 6, 8, 13, 17, 19, 20

tropical rain forest 8, 10, 13, 14, 17

vines 17

Online Resources

Booklinks
NONFICTION NETWORK
FREE! ONLINE NONFICTION RESOURCES

To learn more about plants of the rain forest, please visit **abdobooklinks.com** or scan this QR code. These links are routinely monitored and updated to provide the most current information available.